BASKETBALL
SUPERSTARS
2016

SCHOLASTIC

Photos ©: cover background and throughout: Dewitt/ Shutterstock, Inc.; cover main: Vasilyev Alexandr/ Shutterstock, Inc.; back cover: Dan Thornberg/Shutterstock, Inc.; 1: Sue Ogrocki/AP Images; 2-3: Gerald Herbert/Ap Images; 4 top and throughout: Dejan Popovic/Shutterstock, Inc.; 4 bottom left and throughout: Milos Kontic/Shutterstock, Inc.; 4 bottom right and throughout: www.BillionPhotos.com/ Shutterstock, Inc.; 5: Eric Gay/AP Images; 7: Tannen Maury/ EPA/Newscom; 9: Charles Rex Arbogast/AP Images; 11: Gerald Herbert/AP Images; 13: John G. Mabanglo/EPA/ Newscom; 15: Jim Mone/AP Images; 17: Sue Ogrocki/AP Images; 19: Charles Krupa/AP Images; 21: Curtis Compton/ TNS/Newscom; 23: Darren Abate/AP Images; 25: Chris Szagola/AP Images; 27: Chris Carlson/AP Images; 29: Alex Brandon/AP Images; 31: Sue Ogrocki/AP Images; 32 top left: Jim Mone/AP Images; 32 top right: David J. Phillip/AP Images; 32 bottom left: Christopher Szagola/AP Images; 32 bottom right: Stephen M. Dowell/TNS/Newscom.

Designed by: Rocco Melillo
Photo Editor: Cynthia Carris

ISBN 978-0-545-90374-5

10 9 8 7 6 5 4 3 2 1   16 17 18 19 20
Printed in the U.S.A.   40

First edition, January 2016

Table of Contents

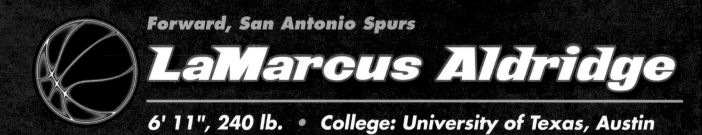

Looking at LaMarcus Aldridge, you'd probably think, "Big guy, inside game, rebound machine." You probably wouldn't think, "Jump-shot artist, deadly mid-range shot." But that's what he is—one of the best "big man" shooters in the NBA. LaMarcus has improved year after year to earn All-Star selections every season since 2012.

LaMarcus comes from a family of basketball stars. For a while, however, it looked like he'd be the brother watching from the stands instead of playing—he was on the shorter side until a growth spurt in junior high. After that, he became one of the top players in his home state of Texas. He stayed home to play for the University of Texas, Austin. There he developed a reputation as a tough defender while also learning the great shooting touch that has made him a star.

The Chicago Bulls made the Longhorns hero the second overall pick of the 2006 NBA draft, but traded him immediately to Portland. For his first few seasons, LaMarcus didn't get a lot of help. The team struggled, only making the playoffs three times and even then never getting out of the first round.

In the 2012–13 season, guard Damian Lillard joined the team, and Portland surprised many by reaching the Western Conference semifinals the following season. LaMarcus, meanwhile, had established his All-Star skills for all to see.

In 2014–15, he suffered an injury to the thumb on his left hand. For most players, that would mean a trip to the operating room or at least some time on the sidelines to heal. But LaMarcus knew what he meant to his team and knew how much they needed him. He decided to save surgery for the off-season and stay in the game. Wearing a brace on his hand, he helped Portland win 51 games and earn its second straight playoff spot. He also set a career high with 23.4 points per game, the highest on the team, while also hauling a team-high 10.2 rebounds per game. Though his hand bothered him all the time, not playing would have bothered him more.

With the hand healed over the summer, LaMarcus decided that he would leave Portland and join the San Antonio Spurs. Playing beside Tim Duncan, LaMarcus hopes to put a ring on that hand in 2016.

3 POINTS

- *Has led the NBA in two-point field-goal attempts each of last three seasons*

- *Has averaged 20-plus points per game five straight seasons*

- *Named top defender in the Big 12 as a sophomore at Texas*

BIG Game!

Named an All-Star starter for the first time in 2015, LaMarcus scored 18 points. In three previous All-Star games, he had combined for only 8!

LaMarcus Aldridge

Giannis Antetokounmpo

6' 11", 217 lb.   College: None

Not very long ago, Giannis Antetokounmpo had never heard of the NBA draft, had never tasted peanut butter, had never been on an airplane, and had made money selling toys and candy on the streets of Athens, Greece. Today, he's one of the NBA's hottest young stars, the best player on the Milwaukee Bucks, and a huge fan favorite thanks to his winning attitude. The story of the guy they call the Greek Freak is one of the coolest in sports.

Giannis was born in Greece to parents who emigrated from Nigeria. They struggled to find work, so Giannis and his brothers had to help the family. Often, they would sell things on the street, including candy, toys, and watches. Giannis's height and athletic ability was put to use on the basketball court, where he slowly developed his game. In Greece, there is no high school basketball. Instead, players play for clubs, quickly becoming pros if they're good enough.

While playing in the Greek pro league against players sometimes twice his age, his skills shone through. The NBA looks all over the world for players, and scouts saw something special in Giannis. Several teams wanted him, but the Bucks chose him with the 15th pick of the 2013 NBA draft. Giannis had only learned about the draft a couple of years earlier; he had thought NBA teams just took whomever they wanted.

Giannis arrived in Milwaukee and spent almost as much time learning how to live in the United States as he did playing hoops. He studied for a driver's license. He learned how to send money home to his parents. He tried lots of new food, including peanut butter. He tried to learn about taxis but sometimes got rides to games from fans and fellow teammates.

But on the court, he was right at home. His slashing moves to the basket and his fearless, acrobatic play earned his nickname: the Greek Freak! In 2015, he nearly doubled his per-game scoring. The Bucks made the playoffs and went six games against a gritty Chicago Bulls team. Even though the Bucks didn't make it past the first round, Giannis was a bright light for them. Think how good he'll be once he learns more!

3 POINTS

- Played in the 2013 Greek League All-Star Game
- Brother Thanasis was drafted by the Knicks in 2014
- Played for Greece at the 2014

BIG Game!

In only his second month in the NBA, Giannis put together his first double-double. He scored a season-high 16 points and grabbed 10 boards in a Bucks' loss to the Brooklyn Nets.

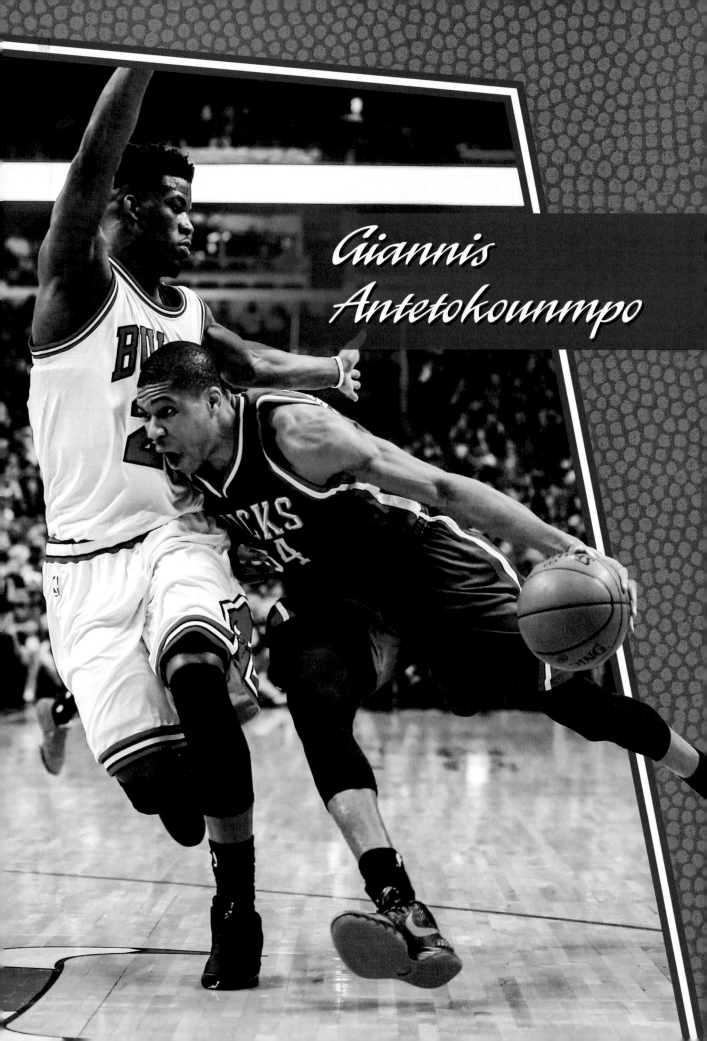

Giannis
Antetokounmpo

Jimmy Butler

6' 7", 220 lb. • College: Marquette University

At the rate Jimmy Butler is improving, the whole league better watch out! Starting his fifth NBA season, Butler has transformed from a third-stringer into one of the league's best. He chalks it up to one thing: hard work.

Butler grew up in Texas but had a hard life as a youngster. Things were so bad that his mom threw him out of their house when he was just thirteen. He was homeless for a time before finding a place to stay with friends and basketball teammates. He was eventually taken in by a family that already had seven kids. Though it was a struggle, he graduated high school and then played in junior college. A move to Marquette University in 2008 showed Jimmy that he might really have a future in the game.

He was among the Big East Conference's top players. Chicago picked him at the end of the first round of the 2011 NBA draft. That's when Jimmy started his step-by-step journey up the ladder. First year: hardly played at all. Second year: played more, scored more, and put on a show in the Bulls' run to the Eastern Conference semifinals. Third year: became a starter and a defensive stopper. Fourth year: All-Star, team's leading scorer, playoff stud. See why everyone should watch out?

That fourth season, 2014–15, was Jimmy's real breakout. He led the Bulls with a 20-points-per-game average, while leading the NBA with 38.7 minutes played per game. He saw his numbers in other areas continue to get better, too—in assists, rebounds, and shots taken. Bulls' fans were not the only ones to notice. In May, Jimmy was named the NBA's Most Improved Player. The way he's going, he'd better make room in his trophy case for some more hardware soon!

3 POINTS

- Led NCAA with 135.4 offensive rating in 2010
- Nicknamed Jimmy Buckets
- Helped Bulls reach playoffs each of first four seasons

BIG Game!

Jimmy scored a career high with 35 points in a big win over the New York Knicks in December 2014. He also had 7 assists and 5 rebounds!

Jimmy Butler

Guard, Golden State Warriors

Stephen Curry

6' 3", 190 lb. • **College: Davidson College**

Now THAT'S a season to remember! All Stephen Curry did in 2014–15 was once again lead the NBA in three-point shots, lead the NBA in free-throw percentage, carry the Warriors to a team-record 67 wins, and introduce his daughter as a media superstar.

Oh, he was also named the NBA MVP and led Golden State to their first championship since 1975!

The title run was just the latest success in Curry's climb to the top. He grew up in North Carolina watching his dad, Dell, enjoy a long NBA career. Though considered undersized for college ball, Stephen was named All-American while helping little Davidson College reach the Elite Eight, setting an NCAA record for three-pointers. He was the seventh overall pick by Golden State in 2009 and quickly established himself as a three-point superstar. By 2013, he had set the NBA single-season record with 272 buckets from outside the arc. He set a new record in 2014–15 with 286 long-range bombs.

That record was part of an amazing season for Curry. The Warriors burst out at the start, winning 21 of their first 23 games. Curry was burying threes at a record pace. Along with Curry, Golden State boasted offensive firepower from Klay Thompson and Andre Iguodala. The team was led by rookie coach Steve Kerr—a former three-point hero himself.

Golden State rolled through the season, ending with the NBA's best overall record of 67–15. In the playoffs, they lost only three games while beating the Pelicans, Grizzlies, and Rockets. On the way to the NBA finals, Curry's family was an ever-present part of his life. His daughter Riley lit up postgame news conferences with her smile and her antics. His father, Dell, was often shown on TV cheering on his son.

In the NBA finals, Golden State had to take on LeBron James and the Cleveland Cavaliers. The team was up to the task, sharing the defensive load against James. The teams split the first two games (both went to overtime!) in what was quickly becoming an all-time classic finals. Curry caught fire in the series, leading Golden State to a win in six games. The MVP had another trophy to carry around! The only reason he put down the gleaming golden statue of a net and ball was to pick up Riley and celebrate!

3 POINTS

- *Lived briefly in Canada while Dad played for the Toronto Raptors*

- *Takes as many as one thousand shots at the basket before every practice*

- *Helped the US win world championship gold medals in 2010 and 2014*

BIG Game!

In a romp over the Dallas Mavericks in February, Curry set season highs with 10 three-point shots (on 16 attempts) while scoring 51 points!

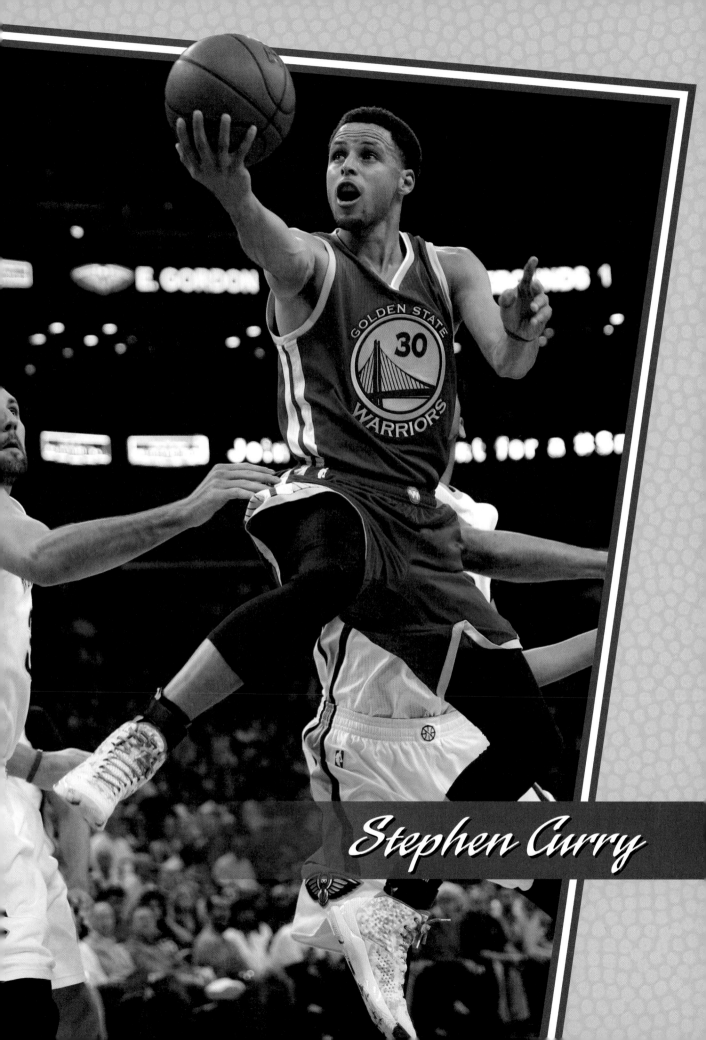

Stephen Curry

Forward/Center, New Orleans Pelicans

Anthony Davis

6' 10", 220 lb. • **College: University of Kentucky**

Everyone around the NBA could see it coming. After all, Anthony Davis had been a star since he sprouted seven inches in one year in high school. Growing up in Chicago, he was one of the top high school players in the country. His long arms and quick feet made him a defensive powerhouse. At the University of Kentucky, he became a shot-blocking wizard, helping the Wildcats win the NCAA championship in 2012.

He was the first overall pick of the 2012 NBA draft by New Orleans. By his second season, he was leading the NBA in blocks.

So everyone had seen how good Anthony was . . . but they also knew that once he figured out the NBA, he'd be even better. Maybe even the best.

And in 2014–15, he figured it out. Not only did he lead the NBA in total blocks and blocks per game, he scored a career-high 24.4 points per game, good for fourth in the NBA. He also was first in two-point baskets made. When you have a wingspan that reaches seven feet four, you can soar above the crowd for dunks and tip-ins.

Along with his numbers, Davis had a new sense of leadership on the Pelicans. He was no longer the youngster; he was a veteran. He grabbed that role, made his second All-Star team, and earned a spot on the All-NBA team as well. He sure has figured it out.

By the end of the regular season, he was matching some of the all-time greats in newfangled stats, like player efficiency rating. Anthony's 2014–15 mark of 30.8 trailed only names like Michael Jordan, LeBron James, and Wilt Chamberlain on the all-time list.

Plus, along with his individual success, Anthony led the Pelicans to team success. New Orleans made the playoffs for the first time with Davis on the team, and their 45 wins were the most since he joined them. Though they lost to the Golden State Warriors in the first round, it was a huge step forward for the wide-winged young superstar.

3 POINTS

- *Set an NCAA record for blocks in a season as a freshman*
- *Named Most Outstanding Player of 2012 NCAA Final Four*
- *Nicknamed The Brow because of his unique facial hair*

BIG Game!

In a March 2014 win over the Boston Celtics, Anthony had season highs in both points (40) and rebounds (21) while also blocking 3 shots and having only 1 turnover!

Anthony Davis

Center, Memphis Grizzlies

Marc Gasol

7' 1", 265 lb. • College: None

Big NBA players from outside the United States play a different game than those born stateside. Look at German star Dirk Nowitzki, who has one of the best outside shots in the league. Or check out the talented Argentine player Manu Ginobili, who is big and quick. Spain's Pau Gasol can power inside but also shows off a great shooting touch.

The Gasol family boasts more than just the two-time NBA champion Pau. Younger brother Marc Gasol has powered the Memphis Grizzlies to the top ranks of NBA teams since he joined them in 2008. Marc has a strong defensive presence—he's won the Defensive Player of the Year award. On the offensive end, at 7'1" he can actually reach over most defenders to pour in sweet jumpers.

The Gasols grew up in Spain and were among the country's best players. Both have helped Spain's national team in the Olympics and the World Cup. Pau reached the NBA in 2001; Marc was drafted with the 48th pick by the Los Angeles Lakers in 2007. A year later, the brothers were actually traded

for each other. Pau headed to LA, where he helped the Lakers win two titles. Marc moved to Memphis.

He soon teamed with fellow big-body Zach Randolph to give new life to a down team. By 2011, the Grizzlies were in the playoffs, and they've made it every year since. In 2014–15, Marc and Memphis had their second-best record ever. For most of November, they had the NBA's best record. The team started the season winning 15 of its first 17 games. The Grizzlies didn't lose its tenth game until January!

Some experts pointed to work Marc had done in the off-season. He's always been a big guy, but heading into the 2014 season, he was less of a big guy. Hard work in the off-season had trimmed some pounds, which made him lighter and quicker. He ended up with a career-high 17.4 points per game.

In the 2015 playoffs, Marc led the team to a first-round win over Portland, scoring a team-high 26 points in the clincher. Though Memphis lost to super-hot Golden State in the semifinals, the Grizzlies and Marc are sure to roar again!

3 POINTS

- Helped Spain win European Championship twice
- Won 2013 NBA Defensive Player of the Year
- Ranked with brother Pau as best brother tandem in the NBA

BIG Game!

In a 2015 win over the Indiana Pacers, Marc was dominant at both ends. He scored a season-high 33 points while pulling down 13 rebounds.

Marc Gasol

James Harden

6' 5", 225 lb. • College: Arizona State University

Fear the beard! James Harden's NBA opponents know that it's not his famous beard that beats them, it's his pinpoint shooting, great court sense, and determination that make him a winner.

In college at Arizona State, he was the Pac-12 Player of the Year and one of the top players in the nation. After two seasons, the Oklahoma City Thunder made him the No. 3 pick in the 2009 NBA draft.

As good as he was in college, James had a hard time establishing himself in the NBA. He rarely started for the Thunder. The team ran through big man Kevin Durant, and Harden was stuck behind other stars such as Russell Westbrook. However, he had found his spot. By coming off the bench as a boost of energy for his team, he helped them more than if he had been starting. After the 2011–12 season, he was named the top Sixth Man in the NBA.

That was a big honor, and James hoped to continue to help the Thunder improve. But he was traded to the Houston Rockets before the 2012–13 season. While the Thunder was on the way up, the Rockets had not made the playoffs in three seasons. However, with Houston, James would finally be the go-to guy.

He set a career-high by scoring 25.9 points per game to lead the Rockets, and he's been scoring buckets in buckets ever since!

In his first season with Houston, they returned to the playoffs and have made it every year since. In 2014, he was named to the All-NBA First Team. In 2014–15, no one played more minutes than Harden did. He was second in the NBA in scoring with a career-high 27.4 points per game and finished second in the NBA MVP voting to Stephen Curry. Plus, he helped his teammates by finishing sixth in the NBA in total assists.

During the 2015 NBA playoffs, Harden led the Rockets to a stirring comeback against the Los Angeles Clippers. Trailing 3–1 in games, Houston won three straight to stun LA. Harden poured in 31 points in the clinching Game 7.

Unfortunately, not even Harden's beard was enough to overcome the scoring power of Curry and the Golden State Warriors in the Western Conference finals. However, the Rockets should continue to soar as long as Harden doesn't shave!

3 POINTS

- Selected First-team All-American as a senior
- Played for the United States in 2012 Summer Olympics
- Led NBA in free throws made, with 715 in 2014–15

BIG Game!

He couldn't miss! In an April 2015 win over the Sacramento Kings, James poured in a career-high 51 points. He made 8 of 9 three-point attempts and 11 of 13 free throws, plus had a .640 field-goal percentage. Wow!

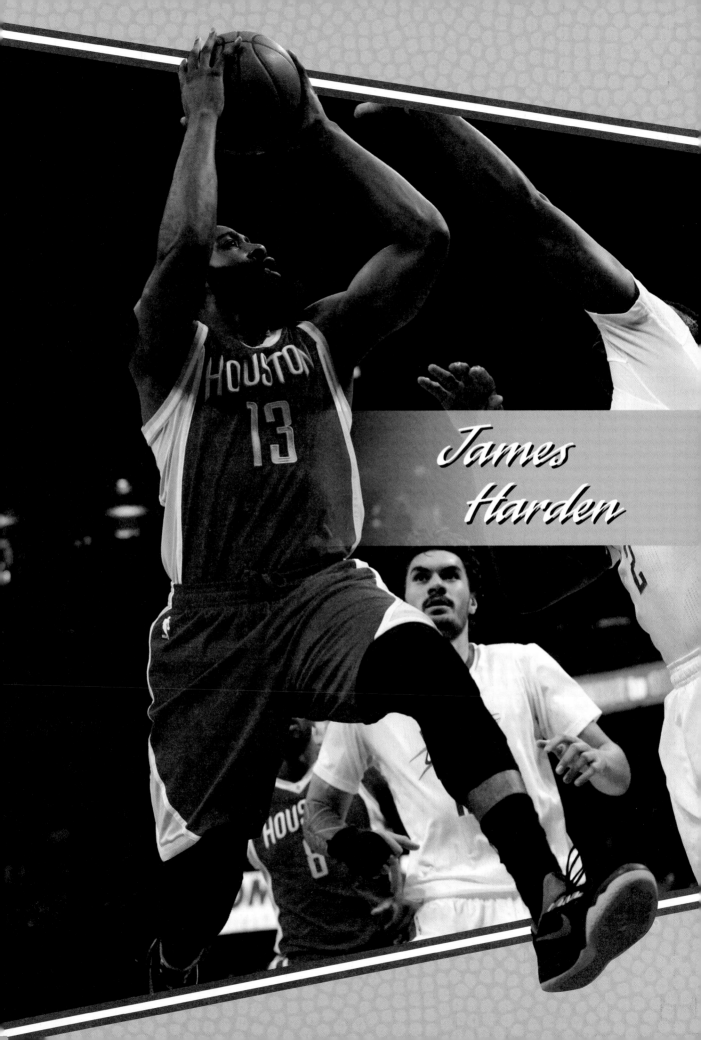

James
Harden

LeBron James

6' 8", 250 lb. • College: None

Since basketball was invented way back in 1891, it's always been five versus five. In the 2015 NBA Finals, it was pretty much one versus five…and the one nearly pulled it off. With key injuries to his All-Star teammates Kyrie Irving and Kevin Love, LeBron James single-handedly carried the Cleveland Cavaliers in the championship round but in the end couldn't win it all. It was not for lack of trying. After he dominated play in the six-game series, some people called for him to be the Finals MVP—even though his team lost!

The people of Cleveland certainly agreed. The 2014–15 season was LeBron's return to his hometown after four years with the Miami Heat. LeBron had his pick of NBA cities after his time with the Heat was up. But he chose the place where he had grown up (in Akron, actually, not far from Cleveland). As a teenager, he had been the top player in Ohio and one of the best in the nation. He was so talented, he skipped college ball and went right to the NBA. He was the first overall pick by Cleveland in 2003.

He wasted no time piling up the hardware, winning Rookie of the Year. He added a pair of All-Star Game MVP trophies and was twice the NBA MVP while with the Cavs. In 2010, he stunned his fans by making "The Decision" to move to Miami. Once there, he teamed with Dwyane Wade and Chris Bosh to form a dominant threesome that won two NBA titles for the Heat.

The Cleveland area welcomed him back with open arms—not a surprise considering LeBron is widely considered to be the Best Player on the Planet. He's now appeared in five straight NBA finals—six total in his career.

LeBron was the first player ever to lead the finals in points, rebounds, and assists per game. He scored 38.3% of Cleveland's points, the second-highest mark ever. He had a 40-point triple-double—double digits in three separate stats—in Game 5—the first in a finals in thirty years.

With the return of Irving and Love, and with LeBron continuing to be the king, next year he might bring that title home to Cleveland, too.

3 POINTS

- *Known for scoring but named to NBA All-Defensive Team six times*
- *Led NBA in field goals four times*
- *Led in Player Efficiency Rating (PER) six times*

BIG Game!

It's hard to pick one from his amazing career, but let's go with LeBron's triple-double in Game 5 of the 2012 NBA Finals. He scored 26 points, had 13 assists, and pulled down 11 rebounds as he won his first NBA title with Miami over Oklahoma City.

LeBron James

Kyle Korver

6' 7", 212 lb. • College: Creighton University

The Atlanta Hawks was one of the biggest stories of the 2014–15 NBA season. None of the team's players were megastars, but the combination of all-around talents and unselfish play helped them to the Eastern Conference's best regular-season record.

The month of January sealed the deal for the Hawks. The team had the best single month by a team in NBA history, winning 17 games while losing none! One of the most important weapons in the Hawks' rise to the top was the sharpshooting Kyle Korver.

In his third season in Atlanta and his twelfth in the NBA, Kyle continued to show off the three-point skill that has kept him on the court. His .492 three-point percentage was the best in the league for the second season in a row (and third time overall).

Kyle has always been a top shooter. Maybe he gets it from his mom, a high school star who once scored 73 points in a game! Or from his dad, who was a college basketball player. Or maybe it's just from tons of practice. Wherever it comes from, Kyle's outside shooting skills fit perfectly in Atlanta's plan.

After starring at Creighton University in Nebraska, he was drafted by the New Jersey Nets in the 2003 NBA draft but traded to the 76ers on draft night. By his second season, he led the NBA with 226 three-pointers. He moved to the Utah Jazz during the 2007–08 season and was top in the league in "trey" percentage in 2009–10. After two seasons with the Chicago Bulls, he joined Atlanta in 2012. Though he had not been a starter since 2006, the Hawks put him into their first five, and the move paid off.

In 2015, Atlanta made it to its first Eastern Conference final, and Kyle was named to his first All-Star team (along with three other Hawks players).

But even Korver's pinpoint shooting was not enough to overcome LeBron James and the Cavs. Still, it was a remarkable season for the Hawks, with a big thanks to Korver's ability from long distance.

3 POINTS

- *Twice led Missouri Valley Conference in three-point and free-throw shooting percentage*

- *Led NBA in free-throw percentage (.914) in 2006–07*

- *Won NBA Sportsmanship Award in 2015*

BIG Game!

During a win over the Bulls during the Hawks' amazing January, Kyle buried a season-high 7 three-pointers and added 3 free throws for a team-high 24 points.

Kyle Korver

Forward, San Antonio Spurs

Kawhi Leonard

6' 7", 230 lb. • **College: San Diego State University**

On a team packed with superstars, a young player emerged in 2014 to be the biggest star of all. Kawhi Leonard was the surprise winner of the 2014 NBA Finals MVP award after he helped the Spurs win their fifth NBA title.

Kawhi grew up near Los Angeles and was a tall, strong player in high school. As the top player in the state, he was named California Mr. Basketball in 2009.

Kawhi played two years at San Diego State, where he became one of the school's best players ever. As a sophomore, he helped the team win its first-ever NCAA playoff game.

In 2011, he was drafted in the first round by the Indiana Pacers but was immediately traded to the San Antonio Spurs. There he joined one of the NBA's most experienced teams. Kawhi got to learn firsthand from Tim Duncan, Tony Parker, and Manu Ginobili, along with future Hall of Fame coach Gregg Popovich. Kawhi didn't try to become a star. Instead, he wisely fit his power game and tough defense into the Spurs' successful system. He tried to just get better year after year.

By the 2013–14 season, he was starting nearly every game he played in and helping at both ends. The Spurs roared to a 62-win season. They beat the Mavericks, Trail Blazers, and Thunder in the playoffs. That set up an NBA Finals matching the veteran Spurs against the Miami Heat.

San Antonio's defense, led by Kawhi, shut James down for the most part. The teams split the first two games, and then Kawhi took off. He scored 29, 20, and 22 points in the next three games, all of which San Antonio won. The young player's surprise success stunned fans and the Heat alike. San Antonio won in five games, and Kawhi was the easy choice for Finals MVP at the age of 22!

How do you follow up a big award like that? Win another big award for a full season of success! Kawhi was named the 2014–15 NBA Defensive Player of the Year for his fierce ability to shut down opposing shooters.

BIG Game!

3 POINTS

- *Tied San Diego State record for career double-doubles*

- *Has improved per game averages in points, rebounds, and steals four straight seasons*

- *Led NBA in steals per game with 2.31 in 2014–15*

Kawhi's biggest game was a big one for the Spurs, too. Tied 1–1 in the 2014 NBA Finals, San Antonio was on the road at Miami for Game 3. A loss would put them in a big hole. Kawhi made sure they went home happy by scoring 29 points and putting the Spurs on the road to another title.

Kawhi Leonard

Guard, Toronto Raptors

Kyle Lowry

6' 0", 205 lb.   College: Villanova University

Kyle grew up in Philadelphia, which has long been a hoops hot spot. After starring in high school there, he played college ball at nearby Villanova University. After two solid years, he felt like he was ready for the pros. The Memphis Grizzlies took him in the first round of the 2006 NBA draft. However, Kyle couldn't crack the starting lineup. He was a solid backup, but not the star he knew he could be. He was traded to Houston during the '08–'09 season.

He was on the bench at first for the Rockets, too. Finally, in 2011, he became a starter and set a then career high with 14.3 points per game. He was now more valuable, but the Rockets sent him to Toronto in a 2012 trade.

In a country known more for ice hockey, Kyle finally found his home. He jumped into the starting lineup, and the Raptors made the playoffs in 2014. In that postseason, Kyle gained the attention of many NBA experts with his performance against Brooklyn. He rallied the underdog Raptors to within seconds of a seven-game win. They lost, but the series gave Kyle and the team a huge boost.

After that great performance, Kyle was a free agent. He could have left for a new team. Several top NBA teams were ready with a big contract. Kyle was torn. Some of those teams were closer to the NBA Finals than the Raptors. They play in bigger US cities, while the Raptors are in a different country.

But Kyle looked at what he was building up north. He saw a great teammate in backcourt mate DeMar DeRozan. Kyle thought that he "may not ever get a chance to say it's [my] team again. Take advantage of it." The Raptors locked him up with a four-year deal.

In 2014–15, Kyle used his newfound confidence to help the Raptors have their best season yet. He was elected to his first starting spot in his first NBA All-Star game, thanks to a nationwide campaign among Canadian fans.

The Raptors set a team record with 49 wins and finished first in the Atlantic Division. Though they were swept by the Washington Wizards, the Raptors know they have more playoffs in their future now that Kyle is on their side.

3 POINTS

Overcame major knee injury during college career

Got the first of his seven career triple-doubles in 2011

His Lowry Love Foundation helps kids in need in Philadelphia & Toronto

BIG Game!

With DeRozan out in December 2014, Kyle took over the offense. He scored a personal season-high 39 points as the Raptors continued the hot start and beat the Jazz.

Kyle Lowry

Guard, Los Angeles Clippers

Chris Paul

6' 0", 175 lb.   College: Wake Forest University

Sometimes it just takes the right setting for a player to really shine. Chris Paul has been a superstar almost since he stepped onto the court as a young player in North Carolina. But it was not until he arrived in Los Angeles in 2011 that the hoops world realized just how special a playmaker he is.

After high school, Paul stayed in his home state and attended Wake Forest University. Playing in the tough Atlantic Coast Conference, the Demon Deacons loved their lightning-quick point guard. Paul was the 2004 ACC Rookie of the Year and in his second season carried his team into the NCAA tournament.

By 2005, he felt that he was ready for the NBA . . . and he was right. After being drafted by the New Orleans Hornets and averaging 16.1 points and 7.8 assists per game, he was the 2006 NBA Rookie of the Year. Although he led New Orleans to two playoff spots, he was overshadowed by guards who played on more popular teams. At only six feet tall, he did not tower over other players but used his quick hands to make perfect passes or slither through traffic to the hoop.

Meanwhile, Paul also excelled in the international game. The wider lane and faster pace of international play suits his game perfectly. He didn't even wait for the pros to make his mark, helping the United States win the 2004 World Junior Championship. After joining the NBA, he was twice named to play in the Summer Olympics. In both 2008 and 2012, his sparkling guard play helped the United States bring home gold medals!

In 2011, however, everything changed. Paul joined the Los Angeles Clippers, a team badly in need of a star. The Clips had made the playoffs only once in the previous fourteen seasons. They had had only one winning season since 1993.

Paul, with help from big man Blake Griffin and others, changed that. Since Paul came to the big city, the Clippers have not only had four straight winning seasons but also set a team record in 2014 with 57 wins. The team made the playoffs four times, too, and reached the Western Conference semifinals three times.

The little guard is now playing on the big stage, and the spotlight is showing off his talent as one of the NBA's very best players.

3 POINTS

Named to the McDonald's All-American team as a high school senior

Led NBA in steals five times

Named to eight consecutive NBA All-Star games and was MVP of the 2013 contest

BIG Game!

On the way to the Clippers' fourth straight playoff berth since he joined, Paul had season highs in both points (41—nearly a career high) and assists (17) in an April 2015 win over the Portland Trail Blazers.

Chris Paul

John Wall

6' 4", 195 lb. • College: University of Kentucky

John Wall thought he had basketball figured out. After joining the NBA, however, he discovered that he had a lot more to learn about the game. But John was used to overcoming obstacles. He used his skills, his smarts, and his dedication to become one of the NBA's most exciting players.

John grew up in Raleigh, North Carolina. His family had lots of problems. John made some bad choices and got in trouble. He found comfort on the basketball court, but almost lost that. His behavior was one reason he was cut from a high school team as a sophomore. He moved to a new school, got his act together, and become one of the top young players in the country.

Many colleges wanted him, but he chose Kentucky. As a freshman, he was named the SEC Tournament MVP while helping his team win the conference title. After only one college season, he was ready for another challenge. The Wizards made him the first overall pick in 2010.

From the start, John realized that his speed and skills were not going to be enough in the rough-and-tumble NBA. He got his points and made the assists, but he needed something else. In the 2013–14 season, he put all the lessons from on and off the court together. He was named an All-Star for the first time. He led the Wizards to their first playoff appearance since 2008. The Wizards beat the Chicago Bulls in the first round—only the third time Washington had won a playoff series since 1978! In 2014–15, Wall led the Wizards to 46 wins—also the most since the 1978–79 season!

A hand injury kept John from playing his best in the playoffs, and Washington lost to the Atlanta Hawks in the second round. But the injury will heal, and the Wizards will return, thanks to a youngster who is a leader among the best players in the sport. Wall will be ready to overcome any obstacle in his way.

3 POINTS

- *Named first team All-American in his only college season*
- *Led NBA with 721 assists in 2013–14*
- *Led NBA playoffs with 11.9 assists per game in 2015*

BIG Game!

In a big first-round playoff game in 2015, John scored 26 points and dished out 17 assists as the Wizards beat the Toronto Raptors.

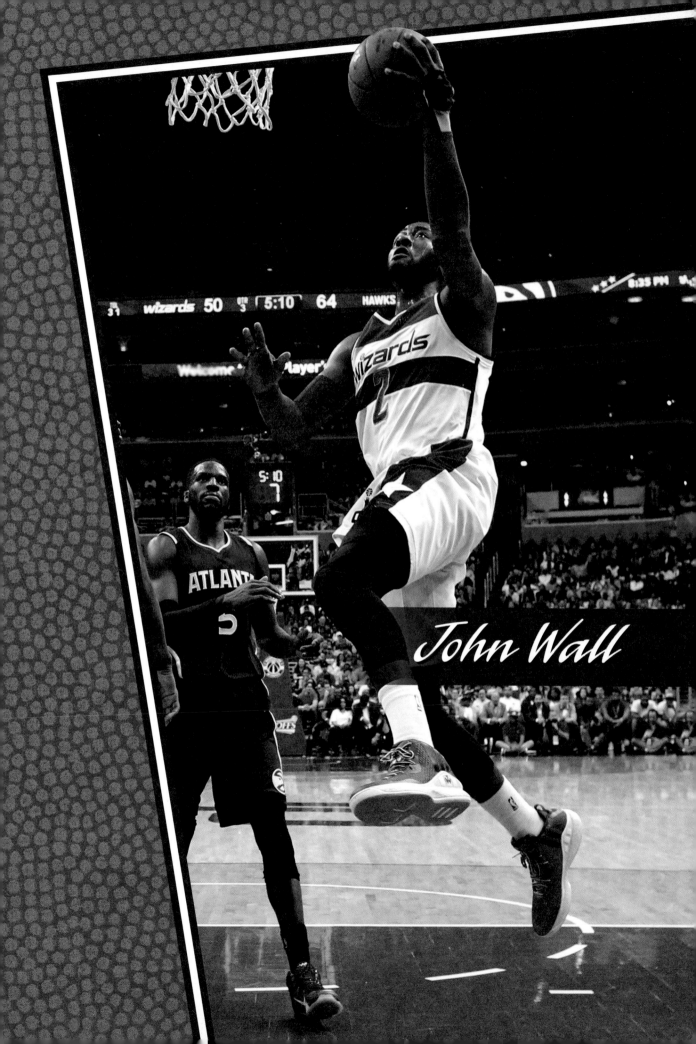

John Wall

Russell Westbrook

6' 3", 200 lb.   **College: University of California, LA**

Talk about a hot streak! For a few weeks in 2015, Russell Westbrook was not just hot... he was on fire! First, he rocked the NBA All-Star game by scoring a game-high 41 points and earning the MVP award. Then he ran off a series of games that stretched into March, racking up points, assists, and rebounds. Over thirteen games, he averaged a triple-double. In four of those games in a row, he had triple-doubles, the first player since Michael Jordan in 1989 with that many.

Did we mention that Russell did all of this while wearing a plastic mask after fracturing a bone in his face?

As amazing as that streak was, it was not a huge surprise. Russell has been putting up amazing numbers and eye-popping highlights since his college days. At UCLA, he was named All-Pac-10 and helped the Bruins reach two straight Final Fours.

Oklahoma City made him the fourth pick of the 2008 NBA draft. With the Thunder, he teamed with Kevin Durant, another superstar. After struggling in their first season together, the two figured it out in 2009–10. The Thunder won 50 games and made the first of five straight playoff appearances.

They had their eye on number six in 2014–15, but Durant played only 27 games after suffering foot injuries. Thanks in part to losing Durant, Russell had to step up and be the main man on the Thunder. Always a scoring machine, Russell did even better that season. His 28.1 points per game was a career high and topped the NBA.

Russell can be proud of that stat win, but he'd trade it for a playoff shot. Without Durant, Oklahoma City just missed earning the eighth spot in the Western Conference playoffs. However, Durant figures to be back in 2015–16. Russell, Durant, and the Thunder will be focused on getting back into the championship hunt.

3 POINTS

- Was just 5'8" in junior high... sprouted to 6'3" as a senior
- Named to 2009 NBA All-Rookie Team
- Led NBA in field-goal attempts and was second in free throws made in 2014–15

BIG Game!

In the middle of his triple-double streak in 2015 was Russell's best game—in a win over the Philadelphia 76ers, he had 49 points, 15 rebounds, and 10 assists! And he even had 3 steals!

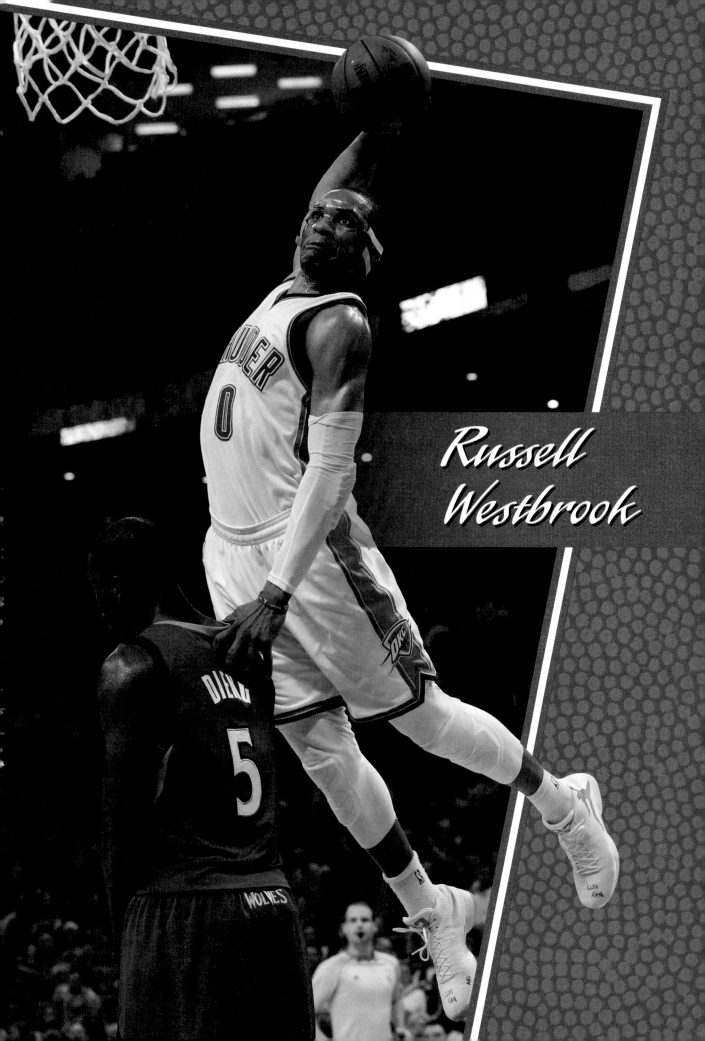

Russell
Westbrook

Here's a look at some players entering their second or third NBA season who will have their eyes on All-Star berths and NBA titles.

Andrew Wiggins was the 2015 Rookie of the Year—the first to hail from Canada! The Minnesota Timberwolves shooting guard led all rookies with 16.9 points per game.

Elfrid Payton was the NBA's rookie leader in assists. A rookie point guard is a rare honor, but the Orlando Magic let Payton have the reins of their offense most of the season. He was named to the NBA's All-Rookie team, along with Wiggins and Noel.

Nerlens Noel of the Philadelphia 76ers actually was in the NBA in 2013–14, but he didn't play a game. A knee injury kept him out of what would have been a rookie season. When he came back healthy for 2014–15, he made that his rookie campaign and excelled. A powerful defender, he was the only player in the NBA's top 10 in blocks and steals, a rare combination. He also led all rookies with 8.1 rebounds per game.

Among second-year players in 2014–15, another Magic man led the way. **Victor Oladipo** averaged 17.9 points per game as well as 1.7 steals, both top among NBA sophomores. The former Indiana University standout joined Payton to give Orlando one of the best young backcourts in the league.